Coming Home to

Vegetarian Recipes Inspired by the Organic

MARY SHEEHAN

Ó Siodacáin

The name Sheehan is the anglicized form of the Irish Ó Siodhacháin, from a diminutive of siodhach, meaning "peaceful." The eponymous ancestor of the family is disputed, but he must have been unique among the Irish of the day to have deserved the description "peace maker." One ancient genealogy has the sept's ancestor as a brother of Brian Boru, while another has him as a member of the Scanlan sept.

Mary Sheehan
County Clare, Ireland

Design and typesetting by Carolyn Evans
Photography by Mary Sheehan, Shay Reyes-Sheehan,
Sinead Corkery, and Carolyn Evans

First Edition

ISBN-978-0-9558768-0-6
PRINTED IN THE REPUBLIC OF IRELAND
by Betaprint

This book is dedicated to my mother, Mary Driscoll Sheehan.

Ó Drisceoil

Acknowledgments

To my dear cousins, the Sheehans and Roches of West Cork and James Curran of Dingle, *go raibh maith agat go deo*, for your kindness and kinship.

To Sadie Chowen and Ralph Doyle of the Burren Perfumery, my appreciation for your vision in creating a lovely oasis in the Burren.

To all my new friends in Ireland, many thanks for filling my first season with warm memories I will keep returning to and coming back for.

Special thanks to Carolyn Evans for layout, technical support and overall generosity and to Sue Hesse for editing and taste testing.

To everyone else who supported me in the conception and creation of this book, you're too many to name, but you know how much you mean to me.

And to my son, Shay, *a buachaill mo álainn*.

Contents

Introduction

I made my first visit to Ireland in the fall of 1977 and stayed for 2 months. I walked a lot of roads, hitchhiked hundreds of miles and heard great traditional music. I met an old Irish-speaking woman in Dingle who knew my grandparents and looked at me with recognition. I remember how the rain felt on my face, how the peat fires smelled and being welcomed by my cousins with a warm glass of poteen and salmon caught that day off Slea Head.

I didn't need to search for my roots, as my grandparents, Dermod Sheehan of Ballyvourney, a traveling teacher for the Gaelic League, and Annie Curran of Dingle, came to America in 1907. In 1956, my grandfather wrote down our family history going back to the 1700s.

On that first visit, I met many Sheehan cousins on their farms in West Cork and the Currans in their pub in Dingle. Thirty years later, they're still there. The dairy farms and the pub are thriving. It's a rare privilege to have a living family legacy in a country that's undergone such radical changes in the past two decades.

I received my Irish citizenship in 2005, found myself with an empty nest and started thinking about living and working in Ireland. In 2007, 100 years after Dermod and Annie came to America to start a new life, I found my way back to the "old country" to start another phase of mine. I accepted a position as manager of the Burren Perfumery tearooms in County Clare. It was the perfect match, an organic vegetarian tearoom in one of the world's unique landscapes.

Whether owning and running Mary's Café in Nyack, New York, or training cooks at a resort in Belize, my job choices have challenged me to focus on locally grown ingredients and thus to create meals that are rich in diversity. The philosophy behind these recipes is a simple one. Prepare fresh, tasty food that makes people feel good, both emotionally and physically. Slow down, simplify and be creative. Whether you're a seasoned cook or just looking for a different dinner option, most of these recipes are easy to follow, delicious and nutritious. Many are dairy and gluten free. Experiment and make them your own. Fresh herbs and vegetables can add zest to tofu and grains. An ordinary-looking dish can be transformed into a work of art with a garnish of colorful fruits, spices and nuts.

If you are lactose intolerant or watching your calories, substitute soy margarine or oil for butter in a soup or bread recipe. If you are gluten intolerant, look for gluten-free pie crusts, flours, breadcrumbs and pasta in the health food store.

Because the names of ingredients and units of measure differ from country to country, I include explanations where they seem appropriate. Please refer to the Conversion Chart on page 81 for dry, liquid, and linear measurements and oven temperatures.

Happy eating!

Mary

The Burren (*Boireann*)

The back road from Carran to Ballyvaughan contains a sampling of everything the Burren has to offer: ancient stone walls, portal tombs, a patchwork of green fields dotted with sheep and cows, a spectacular view of Galway Bay and limestone rock plateaus embroidered with hundreds of varieties of wildflowers peeking out of the grikes. It's not just a landscape, it's a work of art, a magical land clinging to the edge of the Atlantic Ocean. The windswept rocks hold the warmth of the earth, nurturing the spring gentians and summer orchids. Rare species of flora abound.

It was on this road that I stopped one night to experience the solitude of this beautiful place. The soft air embraced me as I looked out over the rocks that glimmered like silver in the ever-changing light of dusk. A wind blew up from the west and carried with it the sounds of the earth and its inhabitants settling for the evening.

Exploring the land, its history and your relationship to it is inevitable here.

There's nothing like a big bowl of steaming hot soup on a cold rainy day. The summer of 2007 was the rainiest on record in Ireland. Despite the rain, it was always a pleasure collecting herbs from the garden in anticipation of the warmth and rich aromas to follow in the tearooms.

All soup recipes serve six, and most are gluten free. Serve any of these with a thick slice of brown bread smothered in Irish butter and a pot of strong tea with rich Irish milk.

Heaven!

Soups

Anraith

Basic Vegetable Stock

A good vegetable stock is essential to making a delicious soup or the base for a sauce or gravy. There are good packaged veggie stocks on the market, but if you want to experiment, start with this recipe and add whatever vegetables you like. I always save the ends of veggies like celery, carrots, peppers and cabbage in the refrigerator to add to a stock, and I save the liquid from steamed vegetables as well. Wash but leave the peel on the vegetables, even the onions and garlic. This stock will keep in the refrigerator for a week and can be frozen for several months in a good plastic container.

3 qt. water
3 medium onions, quartered
6 large carrots, chopped
3 stalks celery, chopped
2 large courgettes (zucchini), chopped
Ends of broccoli and/or asparagus
4 cloves garlic
2 cups mushroom stems
Handful of parsley
2 bay leaves
Sea salt to taste
1 Tbl. black peppercorns

Add all ingredients to water and bring to a boil. Lower the heat, cover the pot and simmer for 1 hour. When cool, strain through a fine-mesh sieve.

Butternut Squash Soup with Crème Fraîche

I have been making this every Thanksgiving for 20 years. It's a great way to start a big meal, as it is light and festive.

    2 large butternut squash, cut into quarters
    2 small sweet potatoes, cut into quarters
    3 Tbl. olive oil
    1 cup diced onions
    1 cup diced celery
    2"-long piece of ginger root, minced
    6 cups vegetable stock
    Sea salt and black pepper to taste
    2 Tbl. honey
    1 tsp. grated nutmeg

Steam squash and potatoes and save liquid. When vegetables are cool, peel, dice and set aside. Heat 3 Tbl. oil. Cook onion, celery and ginger until soft and browned. Add sweet potatoes, squash, stock, salt and pepper. Cook on medium heat for about 30 minutes until veggies are soft. Remove from heat and purée in food processor. Return to pot, add honey and nutmeg and heat for another 10 minutes. Garnish with Crème Fraîche.

Crème Fraîche:
½ cup sour cream
½ cup heavy cream

Mix together and let sit at room temperature until thickened.

Potato Leek Soup with Lovage

This is my version of a classic Irish soup that is very popular at the tearooms. Lovage is a green, leafy plant that is similar in taste to celery. In Germany it is called Maggikraut, in Holland Maggiplant and in Romania Leustean. The leaves are used in soups and tea. We pick our own organic lovage from right outside the door. Can't get any fresher than that!

    10 Tbl. butter
    8 cups diced potatoes
    3 cups chopped leeks
    1 cup chopped lovage
    12 cups vegetable stock
    1 cup light cream
    Sea salt and ground white pepper to taste

In a heavy soup pot, melt 8 Tbl. butter. Add the potatoes and 2 cups leeks and cook until leeks are soft. Add lovage, stock, sea salt and pepper. Bring to a boil, then lower heat and cook for 35 minutes. Blend soup in food processor until smooth. Return to pot and add light cream. Adjust seasonings. In a skillet, melt 2 Tbl. butter and cook 1 cup leeks until soft and brown. Add to soup.

Garnish with sprigs of fresh lovage.

Indian Potato Cauliflower Soup

Here's a nice smooth soup with a little kick.

4 Tbl. butter

½ cup diced shallots

3 garlic cloves, minced

1 cup diced celery

6 cups white potatoes, peeled and diced

6 cups diced cauliflower

2 bay leaves

6 cups vegetable stock

2 14-oz. cans coconut milk

2 tsp. curry powder

1 tsp. ground cumin

½ tsp. cayenne pepper

¼ cup chopped fresh cilantro (coriander)

Salt and pepper to taste

Melt butter. Add shallots, garlic and celery and cook until soft. Add potatoes, cauliflower and bay leaves. Stir ingredients together and cook for 10 minutes. Add veggie stock and bring to a boil. Lower heat and cook for 30 minutes. Remove bay leaves and blend soup in food processor until smooth. Return to pot, add coconut milk, spices and salt and pepper. Cook for another 20 minutes to let flavors combine.

Garnish each bowl with cilantro.

Tomato Fennel Soup with Courgettes

This is a rich-tasting soup that is enhanced by the sweetness of fresh fennel. Courgettes are zucchini, and passata is a thicker version of tomato juice. To tempt the kids, turn this into cream of tomato by adding a swirl of warm milk to each bowl.

2 Tbl. olive oil
½ cup diced onions
½ cup diced green peppers
½ cup diced celery
½ cup diced carrots
2 cups diced fennel bulbs
6 cups tomato passata or tomato juice
4 cups water
3 courgettes, diced small
Fresh fennel leaves
Sea salt and ground black pepper to taste

Heat oil and cook onions and peppers until soft. Add celery, carrots and fennel and cook until beginning to soften. Add passata, water, salt and pepper. Bring to a boil, reduce heat and simmer for 45 minutes. Remove from heat and purée in food processor. Return to pot, add diced courgettes and cook for another 15 minutes.

Garnish with fresh fennel leaves.

Carrot Cardamom Soup

This smooth, delicious soup is an interesting blend of the sweetness of carrots and the bite of turnips. You'll be surprised how this comes to life when you add the spices, cream and a touch of sweetening.

3 Tbl. butter
1 cup chopped leeks
4 cups chopped carrots
4 cups chopped turnips
6 cups vegetable stock
Sea salt and black pepper to taste
1 Tbl. ground cardamom
1 tsp. grated nutmeg
1 cup light cream
¼ cup honey or maple syrup

Heat butter and add leeks, carrots and turnips. Cook until leeks begin to brown and soften. Add stock, salt and pepper. Bring to a boil, lower heat and simmer for 30 minutes. Remove from heat and purée in food processor. Return to pot, add cardamom and nutmeg and cook for 10 minutes. Add cream and honey or syrup and cook for another 10 minutes.

Garnish with chopped curly parsley.

Spring Pea Soup with Mint Pistou

Celebrate spring with this aromatic soup that combines freshly shelled peas and your favorite garden herbs. This is a comforting soup in the winter when you're dreaming of longer days and bright sunshine. You can substitute frozen green peas for fresh and serve this soup hot or cold.

Mint Pistou:
½ cup chopped fresh mint leaves
¼ cup chopped fresh parsley
½ cup olive oil

Blend ingredients and let sit at room temperature while making soup.

Soup:
2 Tbl. vegetable oil
1 cup diced onion

2 cups diced potatoes
2 cups diced celery
2 cups diced carrots
6 cups vegetable stock
3 cups fresh peas
2 bay leaves
1 medium sprig rosemary
Sea salt and ground white pepper to taste
2 Tbl. freshly squeezed lemon juice

Heat oil and add onions, potatoes, celery and carrots and cook until onions are soft. Add vegetable stock, peas, bay leaves, rosemary, salt and pepper. Bring to a boil, lower heat and cook for 30 minutes or until vegetables are soft. Remove pot from heat and discard bay leaves and rosemary. Purée in food processor until smooth. Stir in the Mint Pistou and lemon juice.

Garnish with sprigs of fresh mint.

White Bean Soup with Irish Greens

Your garden in a pot. This is a welcome soup any time of year and makes a complete meal. Serve with a hunk of crusty bread.

2 Tbl. olive oil
½ cup diced onions
2 garlic cloves, minced
½ cup diced celery
½ cup diced carrots
¼ cup diced green peppers
½ cup diced potatoes
½ cup diced courgettes
1 cup thinly sliced mushrooms

3 cups chopped greens (such as kale or swiss chard)
8 cups vegetable stock
3 cups white navy beans
1 Tbl. tomato paste
½ cup chopped fresh basil
1 tsp. chopped fresh thyme
1 tsp. dried oregano
Sea salt and pepper to taste

Heat oil and add all the vegetables in order, stirring well. Cook for 20 minutes or until vegetables begin to soften. Add veggie stock, beans, tomato paste, herbs, salt and pepper. Bring to a boil, then lower heat and cook for 1 hour.

Garnish with fresh herbs and freshly grated parmesan cheese.

Mushroom Barley Soup

A stick-to-your-ribs soup that thickens as it ages. Add more veggie stock as needed for future servings.

Tamari is a darker and richer type of soy sauce. Wheat-free tamari is widely available.

½ cup olive oil
3 garlic cloves, minced
1 cup diced onion
1½ cups diced celery
5 cups chopped button mushrooms
1½ cups washed barley
12 cups vegetable stock
2 Tbl. tamari
2 bay leaves
1 tsp. chopped fresh thyme
Sea salt and white pepper to taste

Heat oil and cook garlic, onions and celery until soft. Add mushrooms and cook until beginning to brown. Stir in barley. Add veggie stock, tamari, bay leaves, thyme, salt and pepper. Bring to a boil, then lower heat and simmer until barley is cooked and soup looks creamy and thick. Remove bay leaves.

Garnish with sprigs of fresh thyme.

Gazpacho

I've lived in and around New Jersey for many years and have always looked forward to the famous glut of Jersey tomatoes each summer. As August 2007 neared and the Irish rain continued unabated, I envied my friends in the northeastern United States who were having picnics at the shore and eating fresh tomatoes like apples. But the organic farmers came through again! My first taste of their beautiful red, juicy tomatoes brought back the sun.

6 large ripe tomatoes, cored and chopped (reserve juice)
1 large red pepper, seeded and chopped
1 large green pepper, seeded and chopped
1 large yellow onion, chopped
2 large cucumbers, peeled, seeded and chopped
1 cup canned tomato juice
½ cup red wine vinegar
1 tsp. cayenne pepper
1 tsp. red pepper flakes
½ cup chopped fresh cilantro
Sea salt and ground black pepper to taste

In a food processor, purée the vegetables, leaving them a little chunky. Remove them from the processor and blend them with the rest of ingredients. Cover and refrigerate to chill and allow flavors to combine. Adjust seasonings for more or less spiciness.

Garnish with sprigs of cilantro.

At the tearooms, visitors often exclaim, "you serve the best salad in Ireland!" Partly that's because we use only locally grown organic vegetables from Dirk and Hella Flake's farm on the Aughinish Peninsula. The rich soil of their rain-swept location and their meticulous care result in superior crops from early spring to late fall.

But it's also the setting of the Perfumery itself—what could be better than sitting at a little table in the garden surrounded by the colors and scents of flowers and herbs, the butterflies fluttering by, the aroma of a rhubarb apple tart baking in the tearooms, the scents of lavender and citrus wafting from the soap-making room?

Have fun with the choices in this section. For a simple but elegant lunch, set the table with a vase of wildflowers and serve a variety of salads with a loaf of homemade bread and a glass of cool crisp wine, followed by a pot of fresh-picked herbal tea and a slice of yummy tart with fresh cream. Make the salad selection by spreading a colorful assortment of greens on a plate. Spoon two or three salads on top of the greens. Add julienned raw veggies like courgettes, carrots, and cucumber, then a few tasty olives and a small round of soft goat cheese. Garnish with edible flowers and sprigs of fresh herbs, and serve with a tasty homemade dressing.

Enjoy!

Salads
Sailéad

Pickled Beets

Whether you juice them, make them into a soup, shred them raw in salads or pickle them, every part of the beet is delicious and high in vitamins and iron. Add beet greens to your lettuce mix, put them in a veggie soup or use them in your soup stock.

You and your guests will be surprised at how tasty this recipe is, considering how few ingredients it uses. A simple and welcome addition to any salad platter.

4 cups sliced cooked beets
6 whole cloves or 2 tsp. ground cloves
1 medium onion, sliced thin
¾ cup cider vinegar
½ cup sugar or ¼ cup honey
½ cup beet liquid
2 Tbl. chopped curly parsley
Salt and pepper to taste

Wash the beets thoroughly to remove any sand, as you will be using the liquid. Cover beets with water, add cloves and cook until beets are tender. Drain, reserve the liquid and slip off beet skins. Slice beets into rounds. Add sliced onion to beets. In a saucepan, blend together vinegar, sugar or honey and beet liquid and bring to a boil. Pour over beets and toss with salt, pepper and chopped parsley. Refrigerate and serve cold.

Burren Roasted Beet Platter

In June, small pink roses cover the tearooms, carpeting the limestone patio with petals. The fennel reaches out its feathery stalks, filling the air with a sweet liquorice scent. Siobhan picks parsley, tarragon and lemon verbena, stopping to pet a kitten napping on the hand-carved rocking chair that welcomes visitors in. The call of the cuckoo competes with the mooing of the cows that graze on hazel bushes on the turlough. It's summer in Ireland and the Burren is in full bloom. This is one of my favorite salad recipes because it is truly locally sourced, simple and fresh. Thanks to my friend, Chef Alex Cormier, for this tasty dressing recipe.

6 large red or yellow beets
Fresh salad greens
Small rounds of soft goat cheese
1 small fennel bulb, sliced thin
2 crisp pears, sliced into thin wedges
¼ cup toasted hazelnuts

Walnut Tarragon Dressing:
1 small shallot, roughly cut
1 cup walnut or hazelnut oil
1 Tbl. sherry vinegar
1 Tbl. spicy mustard
1 Tbl. chopped fresh tarragon
Salt and pepper to taste

Preheat oven to 350°. Trim beets and scrub until free of sand and dirt. Place them in a shallow baking pan filled with about a half-inch of water. Cover and roast for 45 minutes or until tender. Remove from pan, let cool and trim. Slice into rounds. Layer a platter with a variety of fresh greens. Arrange beets in the center. Surround them with goat cheese rounds, fennel, pears and hazelnuts.

In a blender, purée dressing ingredients. Serve dressing on the side.

Garnish with sprigs of fresh tarragon.

Sweet Hot Tofu Salad

Combining the refreshing flavors of summer, this simple salad is tasty, high in protein and low in fat. It goes well on a platter with other salads and works well as a sandwich filling.

    1 lb. tofu, drained
    2 Tbl. vegetable oil
    1 Tbl. freshly squeezed lime juice
    1 tsp. honey
    2 tsp. tamari
    2 garlic cloves, minced
    2 Tbl. diced red onion
    1 tsp. red pepper flakes
    ¼ cup chopped fresh mint
    1 large cucumber, peeled, seeded and diced small
    ½ cup bean sprouts
    Salt and pepper to taste

Cut tofu into bite-size pieces. In a blender, process oil, lime juice, honey and tamari. In a bowl, add these to tofu and mix thoroughly. Add remaining ingredients and toss well. Season with salt and pepper.

Rainbow Spelt

This delicious, highly nutritious salad combines all the colors of the rainbow. Spelt is an ancient grain that is a relative of wheat. It is easier to digest than wheat, so many people who are wheat sensitive are able to tolerate it. It is high in fiber, protein, magnesium, niacin and phosphorus and has a nutty, sweet taste.

2 cups spelt berries, covered with water and
  refrigerated overnight

Finely chop all of the following:
  ½ cup sundried tomatoes
  ¼ cup red pepper
  ½ cup dried apricots
  1/3 cup celery
  2 Tbl. scallions
  2 Tbl. curly parsley
  2 Tbl. golden raisins

White Balsamic Dressing:
½ cup olive oil
1 Tbl. white balsamic vinegar
½ tsp. lemon juice
1 tsp. chopped fresh dill
2 tsp. chopped fresh mint

Drain and boil spelt in 3 cups water for 45 minutes or until soft but still a little crunchy. Mix all the veggies and fruit with the spelt berries. Place dressing ingredients in blender and purée for 1 minute. Pour over salad. Serve cold.

The Miracle of the Cabbage

A favorite story from my grandfather's family history

" Siobhan Ni Loingsigh, my grandmother, was one of the most charitable women in Ballyvourney. At the time of the famine of 1845–1847, she shared her meager supply of food with the poor of the district.

"One day, my grandfather, returning from the fields, noticed that the garden was stripped bare of the last head of cabbage. When he asked my grandmother about it, she said that so many poor people had come to her and that cabbage was the only food left to give them. On his way out the next morning, he was amazed to see that another crop of cabbage had grown up during the night. He called my grandmother to see the miracle. They both went down on their knees, thanking God for this great blessing and miracle. The Sunday after Siobhan died, Father O'Donnell, the parish priest, gave a eulogy on her charity.

"Thank God that most of her descendants have inherited that charity."

Orange Quinoa with Toasted Pecans

The Incas called quinoa "the mother of all grains." It is a gluten-free grain that takes on a pearly appearance when cooked. It is high in protein, iron, magnesium and balanced amino acids, which makes it a complete food.

    1 cup quinoa (2 cups cooked)
    ½ cup toasted pecans
    1/3 cup dried cranberries
    ¼ cup chopped scallions
    2 Tbl. chopped curly parsley
    1 Tbl. chopped fresh tarragon

To cook the quinoa, add it to 2 cups boiling water. Simmer for 15 minutes or until quinoa is shiny and soft.

Balsamic Vinaigrette:
    ¼ cup olive oil
    ¼ cup freshly squeezed orange juice
    1 tsp. balsamic vinegar
    Salt and pepper to taste

Add pecans, cranberries, scallions, parsley and tarragon to quinoa. In a blender, combine all dressing ingredients and purée for 1 minute. Pour over quinoa, mix well and add salt and pepper.

Chill and garnish with sprigs of fresh parsley.

Crispy Tofu Wedges

This is a versatile way to serve tofu that even kids will like. It is very similar to the Spicy Tofu entrée, but the addition of parmesan cheese and nutritional tasty yeast creates a crispy satisfying snack, salad or entrée option.

Nutritional tasty yeast is sometimes called "savory tasty yeast." Its yellow flakes have a strong nutty, cheesy flavor. It is a good source of B vitamins and protein. See the section on Tofu under Meals for the best way to drain and dry tofu. Serve hot or cold. These are great with Sesame Sauce.

1 lb. tofu
1½ Tbl. vegetable oil
½ tsp. each dried basil, oregano, dill and thyme
¼ tsp. each cumin, cayenne and turmeric
1 Tbl. tamari
2 Tbl. grated parmesan cheese
1 Tbl. nutritional tasty yeast
Salt and pepper to taste

Drain tofu. Cut block down the middle and then in half. Slice each half diagonally into 8 triangles. Heat oil and add tofu triangles. Add herbs in order, turning tofu gently to coat. Add tamari and turn to coat. Cook for 2 minutes, carefully turning tofu so triangles don't break. Sprinkle on cheese, coating well, and cook for another 2 minutes. Sprinkle on yeast, mix well and cook for another 2 minutes until tofu is crispy. Season with salt and pepper.

Organic Egg Salad

Spread a spoonful of this on a slice of homemade Irish brown bread and top with thin rounds of cucumber and sprigs of fennel. Serve with a colorful side salad and a light dressing for a delightful lunch.

A helpful hint about peeling hard-boiled eggs—after they're boiled, put the eggs in a bowl, pour very cold water over them and peel immediately. The shells will come right off.

6 extra-large eggs
¼ cup minced red onion
1/3 cup mayonnaise
1/3 cup sour cream
1 Tbl. spicy mustard
1 Tbl. chopped fresh fennel or dill

Hard-boil the eggs. When eggs are boiled, place them in a bowl of very cold water and peel immediately, chop into bite-size pieces in a food processor or mash with a masher. Mix remaining ingredients together and add to eggs. Refrigerate and serve cold.

Harvest Cole Slaw

Colorful and creamy, with tart apples and crunchy walnuts. If you are watching your fat intake, use low-fat sour cream, mayonnaise and yogurt. Make this several hours before serving to let the flavors blend.

1 small green cabbage
2 large carrots, peeled
1 large green apple, peeled and chopped
1 cup chopped toasted walnuts

Creamy Dressing:
2/3 cup sour cream
1/3 cup mayonnaise
1/3 cup plain yogurt
2 Tbl. honey
1 Tbl. white wine vinegar
2 tsp. ground cumin
1 Tbl. chopped cilantro
Salt and pepper to taste

Remove outer leaves of cabbage (save for veggie stock).
Core and cut cabbage into wedges. In food processor,
shred cabbage and carrots. In a big bowl, combine shredded cabbage and carrots with apples and walnuts.
Blend dressing ingredients in another bowl. Pour over salad and mix thoroughly.

Garnish with sprigs of fresh cilantro.

Spicy Cauliflower with Currants

This crisp cauliflower with robust flavors goes well with Hummus and is an excellent accompaniment to the rich color and texture of pickled beets.

    1 large head cauliflower, broken into bite-size pieces
    ½ cup currants
    2 Tbl. capers
    ½ cup chopped kalamata olives
    2 Tbl. chopped red pepper
    2 scallions, chopped
    1 Tbl. chopped Italian parsley
    1 tsp. ground cumin
    ½ tsp. cayenne pepper

Mustard Vinaigrette:
1 cup olive oil
3 Tbl. white balsamic vinegar
1 Tbl. spicy mustard
½ tsp. dried oregano

Steam cauliflower until tender but crisp. Add remaining salad ingredients and mix well. In a blender, purée dressing ingredients in order and blend for 1 minute. Pour dressing over cauliflower and refrigerate for 1 hour before serving.

Garnish with sprigs of fresh oregano.

Hummus

This is a versatile gluten-free dish that I use in sandwiches, as a snack with raw veggies or crackers and as a salad. Garbanzo beans are also known as chick peas. They are a great vegetarian food because they are high in protein, calcium, zinc, fiber and iron and are low in fat. Use them in soups, salads and casseroles. For those who are gluten intolerant, garbanzo bean flour can be used as an alternative to wheat flour. Tahini is a paste made from ground sesame seeds. It is available in raw and toasted forms. I recommend the toasted variety for this recipe.

3¼ cups cooked garbanzo beans
½ cup tahini
¼ cup lemon juice
½ cup water
1½ Tbl. tamari
2–3 garlic cloves, minced
½ tsp. cumin
2 Tbl. chopped parsley or cilantro
Salt and black pepper to taste

In a food processor, purée all ingredients in order, scraping the bowl to incorporate the garbanzos. Add more water as needed to adjust thickness. Serve cold. Makes 3 cups.

Salad Dressings

Use a high-quality oil and fresh herbs for a really superior dressing. The mustard viniagrette from the Spicy Cauliflower with Currants, the White Balsamic from the Rainbow Spelt and the Walnut Tarragon from the Burren Roasted Beet Platter are all delicious dressings that add flavor to a simple green salad. The Creamy Dressing from the Harvest Cole Slaw can be turned into a classic Green Goddess dressing by eliminating the cumin and adding curly parsley. Very Irish, indeed!

My favorite dressing, which I've been perfecting over the past 30 years, is a basic sesame ginger that was my house dressing at Mary's Café.

Sesame Ginger Dressing:
2 cups vegetable oil
1/3 cup tahini
2 tsp. tamari
3 garlic cloves, minced
1½ tsp. ground ginger
2 tsp. spicy mustard

Mix ingredients on low speed in a blender or food processor for 2–3 minutes until thick and creamy. Makes 1 pint.

One of the nicest things about visiting my cousins on their dairy farm in West Cork is arriving in time for dinner, the main meal of the day served at 1:00 pm. There's always room at the table for another guest, and I'm just one of the many who seem to happen by for one of Joan's delicious home-cooked meals. A lovely cup of tea follows. Everyone is talking and laughing, and I'm feeling blessed to be part of this family tradition.

For many of us, it's hard to find time to sit down and share a meal together. From planning to shopping to cooking, it can seem like an overwhelming ordeal. So I've suggested some meals complete with side dishes to make the experience a little easier. Pair these suggestions with a soup or salad and a dessert of your choice, and you've got a really special meal...and maybe the start of your own tradition.

Meals
Beilí

Potato Quinoa Cakes
Serve with Fruit Salsa and Maple Squash with Pumpkin Seeds

My high-protein version of boxty, an Irish potato pancake. I have made these with the hard cheese from the Burren, where the goats nibble on wild herbs and munch on hawthorn and hazel bushes. There's nothing like it!

5 cups cooked mashed potatoes

1½ cups cooked quinoa *(p. 25)*

1 cup diced onion

1 Tbl. butter

½ tsp. paprika

1 tsp. ground cumin

¼ cup chopped parsley

Salt and white pepper to taste

2 eggs, beaten

1 cup grated hard goat cheese or sharp cheddar cheese

½ cup olive oil

½ cup vegetable oil

Peel the potatoes and steam until soft, then mash. Add cooked quinoa to potatoes. After mixing thoroughly, sauté onion in 1 Tbl. butter until soft and add paprika, cumin, parsley, salt and pepper to the onions. Add onions to potatoes, then stir eggs and cheese into the mixture. Form into ten 3" round cakes. Heat olive and vegetable oil in a skillet. Cook cakes on both sides until brown.

Serve topped with Fruit Salsa.

Fruit Salsa

The sweetness of fruit, the crunchy texture of veggies and a little bit of heat make this the perfect accompaniment to a variety of entrées, salads and snacks.

Jicama is a Mexican plant of the legume family. It looks like a turnip, but is crisp and sweet.

2 cups mango or pineapple, cut into small chunks
½ cup jicama or sweet radish, cut into small chunks
¾ cup cucumber, peeled, seeded and diced
¼ cup minced red onion
½ cup diced cherry tomatoes
1 small jalapeño pepper, seeded and minced
¼ cup chopped cilantro
1 Tbl. freshly squeezed lime juice
Pinch of salt

Combine everything in a bowl and refrigerate.

Maple Squash with Pumpkin Seeds

This always gets rave reviews, as it is a welcome change from the standard squash dishes.

1 butternut squash (or fresh pumpkin), cut into 8 pieces
1 Tbl. butter
1 Tbl. olive oil
1½ Tbl. minced fresh ginger root
¼ cup minced shallots
2 tsp. tamari
2 Tbl. chopped scallions
1 Tbl. maple syrup or honey
¼ cup toasted pumpkin seeds
¼ cup chopped curly parsley
Sea salt and black pepper to taste

Steam squash. When tender but still firm, remove from heat and let cool enough to handle. Peel, seed and dice into bite-size chunks. Set aside. Heat butter and oil in a skillet. Add ginger and shallots and cook until browned. Add squash, tamari, scallions, salt and pepper and syrup or honey. Coat well and cook until squash is tender. Remove from heat, put on a platter and garnish with pumpkin seeds and parsley.

Dinner Loaf
Serve with Savory Gravy and Brussels Sprouts with Roasted Garlic

I've experimented with many meatless loaves over the years and keep coming back to this one. The fresh vegetables, crunchy nuts and garden herbs make it a winner. Makes two 9" x 5" loaf pans, each serving 6. This freezes well, whole or sliced.

Bulghur wheat is often called cracked wheat. It is high in protein and fiber and has a higher nutritional content than rice or cous cous. It has a light and nutty flavor.

3 cups cooked bulghur wheat

3 cups cooked short-grain brown rice

3 Tbl. olive oil

1½ cups sliced button mushrooms

1 cup minced onions

½ cup diced celery

½ cup diced carrots

1 cup toasted chopped walnuts

1 cup chopped spinach

1 cup chopped broccoli

4 eggs

2 Tbl. tamari

2 Tbl. catsup

1 Tbl. minced fresh sage

1½ tsp. thyme

1 Tbl. fresh chopped parsley

Salt and pepper to taste

Preheat oven to 350°. Boil 1½ cups water and pour over 1 cup of bulghur wheat. Let sit until dry and fluffy. This will make 3 cups. Mix together bulghur wheat and rice.

In olive oil, sauté mushrooms, onions, celery and carrots until softened and browned. Add walnuts, spinach, and broccoli and cook for three minutes. Add these to bulghur mixture. Beat eggs with tamari and catsup. Add sage, thyme, parsley and salt and pepper. Oil bread pans and add mixture. Optional: add layers of grated sharp cheddar cheese in the middle and on top of loaves. Bake for 45 minutes.

Serve with Savory Gravy.

Savory Gravy

This is one of the best veggie gravies I've made. It's rich and thick, like a good gravy ought to be. For a darker, richer gravy, substitute a French onion soup base for the veggie stock. You can also use butter and white flour if you prefer.

> 3 Tbl. nutritional tasty yeast
> 3 Tbl. soy flour
> 3 Tbl. soy margarine, melted
> 1 Tbl. tamari
> 2 cups vegetable stock or water
> Salt and pepper to taste

Brown the yeast and soy flour in a heavy skillet. Add melted margarine and cook until crumbly. Slowly add tamari, veggie stock or water, salt and pepper. Cook, whisking constantly until smooth and thick. Makes 1 pint.

Brussels Sprouts with Roasted Garlic

> 4 garlic cloves
> 2 Tbl. olive oil or butter
> 2 cups chopped brussels sprouts
> Sea salt and ground black pepper
>   to taste

To roast garlic, leave the peel on, place on a lightly oiled pan and cook at 300° for about 5 minutes.

Melt olive oil or butter. Add brussels sprouts and cook until wilted and brown. When garlic is cool, remove the peel. Chop garlic and add to cooked sprouts. Season with salt and pepper.

Vegetable Torte with Polenta Crust
Serve with Whole Grain Corn Bread

This is a light and beautiful entrée that can be made non-dairy by leaving out the shredded cheese. Use only the freshest herbs and vegetables for a meal that will really make an impression.

2 cups cooked polenta

3 Tbl. olive oil

1 large eggplant, cut into ¼" rounds

3 large portabello mushrooms, thinly sliced

1 cup sliced red onions

1 cup sliced green peppers

2 cups courgettes, cut into ¼" rounds

2 cups sweet potatoes, peeled and cut into ¼" rounds

2 cups chopped spinach

20 asparagus spears, trimmed and cut into 4" lengths

½ cup chopped sundried tomatoes

2 cups fresh tomatoes, peeled and sliced

1 cup chopped fresh basil

6 garlic cloves, roasted and thinly sliced

1½ cups shredded parmesan cheese

Cook polenta according to package instructions. Eggplant contains acidic juices that should be drawn out before cooking. Cut the eggplant into rounds and sprinkle each side with a little salt. Place the slices on a tray lined with a paper towel, top with another paper towel and let sit for 30 minutes. To speed the process, lay a cookie sheet over the tray and place a weight on it. After 30 minutes, rinse off the slices and pat dry.

In a skillet, heat olive oil. Separately sauté eggplant, mushrooms, onions and peppers until each begins to brown. *(Continued on next page)*

Lay on a baking sheet to drain. Separately steam courgettes, sweet potatoes and spinach. Dry spinach thoroughly. Steam asparagus until tender but still crisp.

Preheat oven to 350°. Spray a 9" spring-form pan. Spread polenta over bottom of pan, pressing down to cover evenly. Layer the vegetables in the following order, sprinkling some fresh ground black pepper and a little salt between layers:

> ½ cup grated cheese
> ½ cup basil
> ½ of the eggplant
> All of the onions, peppers and mushrooms,
>   garlic and sundried tomatoes
> 1 cup sliced tomatoes
> ½ cup grated cheese
> All of the courgettes, sweet potatoes and
>   spinach
> The remainder of the eggplant and tomatoes

Lay the asparagus pieces in a circle around the top of the tart with the tips facing inward. Top with the remaining grated cheese

Place torte on a baking sheet and bake for 45 minutes until top is brown and crusty. Note: As the torte is cooking it will loose some of its juice.

Let cool for 15 minutes. Run a knife around the inside of the pan to loosen the torte. Unhinge pan and use a spatula to gently move the torte onto a plate.

Whole Grain Corn Bread

A delicious corn bread that is moist and substantial.

2 cups stone-ground cornmeal
2 cups whole wheat flour
4 tsp. baking powder
1 tsp. baking soda (bread soda)
1 tsp. salt
6 Tbl. melted butter
½ cup honey
2 cups plain yogurt
2 eggs, beaten

Optional:
1 Tbl. chopped cilantro
1 Tbl. minced red pepper

Preheat oven to 375°. In a mixer, combine dry ingredients. Slowly add wet ingredients, mixing well. Beat on medium speed for 1 minute. Pour into 2 greased loaf pans.

Bake for 25–30 minutes until brown on top and a toothpick comes out clean.

The Turf

As you walk through any village in Ireland on a misty night, you still might smell the peat fires burning. Turf holds the history of Ireland in its soggy layers. Jewels, animals once native to Ireland, even butter still white and fresh—all have been uncovered from the ancient bogs. For centuries, turf was the only fuel for cooking and heating. The back-breaking work of cutting it has been replaced by machines, but the picking is still a family tradition.

Mushroom Quiche with Fresh Dill
Serve with Red Potato Salad

Gruyère cheese gives this a distinct flavor that goes superbly with caramelized onions. This is perfect for lunch or dinner. Serve with a couple of light side salads.

3 Tbl. butter

1 large white onion, sliced into long strips

1½ cups button mushrooms, sliced into strips

Pastry Dough *(p. 75)*

1½ cups grated Gruyère cheese

6 eggs

2 cups half-and-half, or 1½ cups light cream plus ½ cup whole milk

Pinch of salt and pepper

1 tsp. chopped fresh dill

Grated nutmeg

Preheat oven to 350°. Melt butter in a skillet and cook onions until caramelized. Add mushrooms and cook 2 minutes. Roll out the Pastry Dough and place it into a 10" pie dish, leaving enough around the edges of the dish to crimp tightly. With a slotted spoon, gently place onions and mushrooms into the pie dish. Top with cheese.

Mix together eggs, cream, salt, pepper and dill. Pour these into the dish, covering the vegetables and cheese. Grate nutmeg evenly over the top. Bake for 45 minutes or until quiche is fluffy and brown. Cut into 8 slices.

Red Potato Salad

A good alternative to a mayonnaise-based potato salad. This is light, delicious and colorful and will dress up any lunch or dinner plate.

12 small new red potatoes, washed, trimmed and cut into bite-size pieces
3 cloves garlic, minced
3 scallions, diced
1/3 cup diced red pepper
¼ cup chopped fresh mint
½ cup olive oil
Sea salt and ground black pepper to taste

Steam potatoes until tender and let cool. Add all other ingredients, mixing gently.

Garnish with sprigs of fresh mint.

Four-Cheese Vegetable Lasagna
Serve with Slammin' Good Garlic Bread and a fresh green salad

This recipe calls for a lot of ingredients, but it is well worth the effort. I have included a layer of fried eggplant, which I think makes this something special, though it can be omitted if you wish. For a gluten-free version, use rice-flour lasagna noodles. One pan serves 6–9.

1 lb. lasagna noodles
1 eggplant, peeled and cut lengthwise into 10 slices
¼ cup plus 3 Tbl. olive oil
1 cup diced onion
3 garlic cloves, minced
¾ cups diced green pepper
1 cup sliced button mushrooms
4 cups whole peeled tomatoes
1 tsp. each dried thyme and oregano
1 cup chopped spinach
½ cup fresh basil

2 eggs
¼ cup milk
½ cup cornmeal mixed with 3 Tbl. white flour or gluten-free flour mix *(p. 68)*
2 cups ricotta cheese
½ cup sour cream
½ cup cream cheese
½ cup shredded fresh parmesan cheese
2 cups shredded mozzarella
Sea salt and ground black pepper to taste

Cook lasagna noodles until tender, stirring occasionally so they don't stick together. Drain, toss with a little vegetable oil and lay on a baking sheet. Tenderize the eggplant slices *(p. 40)*.

Tomato Sauce:
Heat olive oil in a heavy pot. Add onion, garlic, pepper and mushrooms and cook until soft. Add tomatoes, thyme, oregano and salt and pepper. Cook on low heat until tomatoes start to break down, about 30 minutes. Add spinach and basil and cook for 20 minutes more. (*Continued on next page*)

Eggplant:

Beat eggs with milk. Mix together cornmeal and flour on a plate or baking sheet. Wipe eggplant slices dry and dredge them in cornmeal mixture, then egg mixture, then cornmeal mixture again. Fry eggplant slices in a skillet, browning on both sides until soft. Drain and let cool.

Cheeses:

Mix together ricotta, sour cream, cream cheese and parmesan cheese. Add a little salt and pepper.

Assembly:

Preheat oven to 350°. In a 9" x 13" rectangular baking pan, layer ingredients in the following order: sauce, noodles, eggplant, cheese mixture and one third of mozzarella. Repeat, laying noodles in the opposite direction. Finish with a top layer of noodles. Spread with a little sauce and top with remaining mozzarella. Bake for 40 minutes or until lasagna is bubbly and top is browned. Let sit for 15 minutes before slicing.

Slammin' Good Garlic Bread

Thick bread that soaks up the garlic butter is a must for this indulgence.

1 loaf thick whole wheat French bread
½ lb. butter, softened
3 garlic cloves, minced
2 Tbl. chopped parsley
Pinch of salt and pepper

Preheat oven to 350°. Slice bread lengthwise. In a food processor, blend remaining ingredients until smooth. Spread garlic butter on bread, covering completely. Put halves together, wrap in aluminum foil and heat on a baking sheet for 20 minutes. Take bread out of foil and lay halves on baking sheet butter side up. Put the oven on broil and toast bread for a few minutes until crusty and brown. Remove from oven and slice crosswise.

Tofu

Tofu is a compressed form of fermented soybeans that you can find in health food stores, supermarkets and Asian markets. It usually comes in 14- to 16-ounce blocks, which is the correct amount for all of the tofu recipes in this book. Tofu has a bland taste, so the trick to cooking with it is to use lots of herbs and flavorings and to serve it with interesting side dishes.

Because there's a lot of water in tofu, it must be well drained to achieve the correct consistency. The best way to drain a block of tofu is to put it in a fine-mesh strainer and put a weight such as a heavy plate on top of it. To check for dryness, wrap the tofu in cheesecloth or a paper towel and squeeze. Let the tofu drain while you're preparing the other ingredients and side dishes. If a recipe calls for cubes of tofu, be careful that the block doesn't break apart during the draining process.

Tofu Veggie Patties
Serve with Creamy Sesame Sauce, Pasta Pesto, and Cucumber and Fruit Salad

For lunch, serve a tofu patty on a whole grain roll with lettuce, tomatoes, sprouts and Sesame Sauce and some pasta salad on the side. For dinner, start with cucumber salad and serve the Pasta Pesto as a hot dish along with a couple of tofu patties. Makes six 3" patties.

1 lb. firm tofu

2 Tbl. tamari

1 tsp. minced garlic

1 tsp. each dried oregano, basil and thyme

2 Tbl. chopped parsley

2 Tbl. chopped red pepper

2 Tbl. grated carrot

1 Tbl. minced scallions

1/3 cup freshly grated parmesan cheese

½ cup bread crumbs

1 beaten egg

Salt and pepper to taste

½ cup vegetable oil and ½ cup olive oil

In order, add all ingredients except the oils to drained tofu, mixing after each addition. Let sit at room temperature for 10 minutes. Shape into patties, using about a half-cup of the mixture at a time. If the first patty doesn't hold together, add a little more bread crumbs to the mixture. Sprinkle finished patties with additional bread crumbs.

Heat both oils in a skillet. When oil is hot, add patties and cook for 4–5 minutes on each side until brown. Let rest on a paper towel to absorb excess oil.

Creamy Sesame Sauce

I have served this sauce on many varieties of veggie burgers and as a dipping sauce for the Crispy Tofu Wedges (see Salads section). For a healthier version, use non-fat yogurt, sour cream and mayo.

1 cup plain yogurt
½ cup sour cream
¼ cup mayonnaise
¼ cup tahini
1 Tbl. chopped parsley or cilantro
2 Tbl. minced garlic
1½ tsp. tamari
1 tsp. lemon juice
Sea salt and ground black pepper to taste

Place all ingredients in food processor and blend until smooth, about 1 minute. Serve a dollop over a tofu patty and top with a sprig of parsley. Makes 1 pint.

Pasta Pesto

Use a thick noodle to hold up to the pesto and veggies. I like penne or farfalle.

3 cups cooked pasta
1 cup crisp broccoli, steamed and chopped
½ cup sundried tomatoes,
   finely chopped
3 Tbl. chopped scallions

Pesto:
3 cups fresh basil
4 large cloves garlic
1 cup pine nuts
1 cup olive oil
1 cup grated parmesan cheese
Salt and pepper to taste

Let pasta and broccoli cool, then mix together with tomatoes and scallions. In a food processor, blend basil with garlic and pine nuts to form a paste. Slowly add oil, then cheese. Blend for 2 minutes, scraping bowl to incorporate everything. Season with salt and pepper. Mix pesto into pasta, using just enough to coat the noodles. Garnish with sprigs of Italian parsley. Refrigerate remaining pesto for up to 2 weeks.

Cucumber and Fruit Salad

A refreshing, light salad enhanced with fresh mint.

> 1 medium cucumber, cut into thin rounds
> 1 small red onion, cut into thin strips
> 2 small navel oranges, peeled and sectioned
> 1 sweet apple, peeled, cored and sliced thin

When prepared, place the above ingredients in a bowl.

> **Mustard Vinaigrette:**
> ¼ cup olive oil
> 1 Tbl. cider vinegar
> 1 tsp. spicy mustard
> 1 Tbl. white sugar

Blend ingredients and pour over fruits and veggies. Let sit at room temperature until ready to serve. On four individual plates, set out an assortment of greens, such as radicchio, arugula and beet greens, for contrasting colors and flavors. Place a large helping of fruit salad on each plate.

Indonesian Spicy Tofu over Aromatic Jasmine Rice
Serve with Ginger Honey Carrots

The diverse flavors in this entrée make it a wonderful choice for a dinner party. To control the level of heat in this recipe, experiment with the amount of jalapeño seeds and cayenne you add.

Jasmine Rice:
4 cups cooked jasmine rice
3 Tbl. peanut oil
½ cup diced onion
1 jalapeño pepper, diced

1 cup green peas
¼ cup diced red pepper
4 Tbl. tamari
2 Tbl. brown sugar
2 tsp. catsup

Heat oil and add onions, jalapeño, peas, and red pepper. Cook until soft and add to rice. Mix together tamari, sugar, catsup and salt and pepper. Add this to rice, coating thoroughly, and return to stove on low heat.

Spicy Tofu:
2 Tbl. vegetable oil
4 garlic cloves, minced
2 lb. extra-firm tofu, cut into bite-size cubes
1 tsp. each dried basil, oregano, thyme, and dill

½ tsp. each cumin, curry powder, and cayenne
2 Tbl. tamari
Crushed roasted peanuts
¼ cup chopped cilantro
Salt and pepper to taste

Heat oil and cook garlic until soft and brown. Add tofu and cook a few minutes until it begins to brown. Sprinkle dried herbs over tofu and cook 3–4 minutes until tofu is thoroughly coated and starts getting crispy. Add tamari and cook a few more minutes. Serve tofu over rice. Garnish with crushed peanuts and cilantro.

Ginger Honey Carrots

Organic carrots are always tasty when simply steamed and served with a little sea salt and pepper, but why not shake it up with this delicious and easy alternative?

    4 large carrots, peeled and sliced into wedges
    4 Tbl. butter or oil
    1½ Tbl. minced ginger root
    2 Tbl. honey
    2 tsp. tamari
    Sea salt and pepper to taste
    1 Tbl. chopped fresh parsley

Steam the carrots until a little tender but still crunchy. Heat butter or oil, add ginger and carrots and cook until coated, about 2 minutes. Add a little water, cover and steam for 2–3 minutes on high heat. Remove cover, add honey, tamari, salt and pepper and mix well. Cook for another 2–3 minutes until carrots are soft and glazed. Toss with fresh parsley.

Chinese Dumplings
Serve with Broccoli with Peanut Sauce

These are simple and fun to make and good enough for a main course. You'll want 5–6 per person. Dumpling wrappers can be found in Asian markets. For a gluten-free version, substitute rice wrappers for wheat wrappers and wheat-free tamari for hoisin sauce.

Hoisin is a Chinese dipping sauce that is a good flavoring for vegetarian sauces. It contains wheat protein, so if you are cooking for someone who is wheat intolerant, substitute wheat-free tamari.

Sauce:
½ cup vegetable oil
1 Tbl. rice vinegar
1 Tbl. honey
2 Tbl. hoisin sauce
Salt and pepper to taste

Filling for 40 dumplings:
2 lb. tofu, drained and crumbled
40 dumpling wrappers at room
   temperature
2 Tbl. sesame oil
3 garlic cloves, minced
1 medium shallot, diced
12 shiitake mushrooms, diced
3 scallions, diced
1" piece ginger root, minced
1 Tbl. tamari

Prepare the sauce and set aside. Heat oil in a sauté pan or wok. When hot, add garlic and shallots and cook 2 minutes. Add mushrooms, scallions and ginger and cook for 2–3 minutes, turning constantly. Add tamari and cook for another minute. Remove from heat. In a bowl, add cooked ingredients to tofu.

Bring a large pot of salted water to the boil. Sprinkle a cookie sheet with flour or cornmeal. Fill a small bowl with cold water. *(Continued on next page)*

Assembly

Place a wrapper in your left hand, dip the fingers of your right hand in cold water and spread water halfway around top edge of dumpling. Place 1½ Tbl. tofu mixture in center of dumpling. Fold from bottom up, pressing wetted edges together. Lay the dumplings in a row on a plate or cookie sheet, making sure they don't overlap and stick together. When all dumplings are assembled, drop one at a time into boiling water. Cook for a maximum of 2 minutes, remove with a slotted spoon and lay on a platter.

Cover with sauce, 2 Tbl. toasted sesame seeds and ¼ cup chopped cilantro or parsley.

Serve immediately.

Broccoli with Peanut Sauce

This tasty side dish goes well with almost any meal.

> 4 cups chopped broccoli
> 3 garlic cloves, minced
> ¼ cup diced shallots
> 2 Tbl. sesame oil
> 2 Tbl. smooth peanut butter
> 1 cup hot water
> 1 Tbl. tamari
> 1 cup bean sprouts
> Red pepper flakes
> Salt and pepper to taste

Sauté broccoli, garlic and shallots in sesame oil until beginning to brown. Dissolve peanut butter in 1 cup hot water, and mix in tamari to form a sauce.

Pour sauce into skillet and mix until vegetables are coated. Add bean sprouts and stir. Add a sprinkling of pepper flakes, salt and pepper. Cook for a few minutes until everything is blended and broccoli is tender but crunchy.

Tofu Cutlets with Mushrooms, Rosemary and Port Wine Sauce
Serve with Nutty Rice Pilaf and Seared Haricots Verts

A colorful dish that blends the savory taste of mushrooms with the essence of rosemary and the richness of cherries. With the haricots and rice, this meal serves 4–6.

2 lb. firm plain tofu

½ cup plus 2 Tbl. cornstarch

½ cup white flour (or gluten-free flour mix)

Salt and pepper

4 Tbl. olive oil

4 Tbl. butter

4 small shallots, minced

6 cups thinly sliced mushrooms (use a variety)

2 Tbl. minced fresh rosemary

2/3 cup dried cherries

1½ cup vegetable broth

1 cup port wine or cherry juice

1½ Tbl. tomato paste

Drain tofu. When thoroughly dry, cut block in half. Cut each half into 4½"-thick slices. Mix cornstarch, flour, salt and pepper in a shallow bowl. Heat olive oil in a skillet. Dredge tofu slices in cornstarch and flour mixture, coating well. Cook in oil, turning once so cutlets are crisp and golden on each side. Set on a baking sheet and put in oven to keep warm. After tofu is cooked, add butter to the same skillet. Cook shallots until soft. Add mushrooms and cook until lightly browned. Stir in rosemary and cherries and cook for another minute.

In a bowl, mix together vegetable broth, wine or juice and tomato paste. Stir in 2 Tbl. cornstarch. Mix thoroughly and add to skillet with mushrooms. Cook until sauce begins to thicken and becomes glossy. Place cutlets on a platter and pour sauce over them. Garnish with sprigs of fresh rosemary.

Nutty Rice Pilaf

Rice's nutty flavor and texture are perfect with tofu, and the two together make a complete protein. For this recipe, I like to use short-grain brown rice, but a wild rice blend is good, too.

4 cups rice, cooked and cooled
½ cup chopped shallots
2 Tbl. olive oil
½ cup chopped pecans
¼ cup chopped parsley
1 Tbl. chopped fresh thyme

Sauté the shallots in olive oil. When they are transparent, add pecans and sauté for a few minutes until brown. Remove from pan and add parsley and thyme. Mix all ingredients into rice. Cover and keep warm.

Optional:
Dried cranberries and sautéed mushrooms are delicious additions to this pilaf and make it extra special. Use ½ cup of each to 4 cups rice. (You won't want to do this if you're serving the pilaf with the Tofu Cutlets, which contain both ingredients in the sauce.)

Seared Haricots Verts

2 Tbl. olive oil
2 garlic cloves, minced
2 Tbl. minced shallots
4 large button mushrooms, thinly sliced
1 lb. haricot verts or green beans, trimmed
A pinch of sea salt and ground black pepper

Heat oil in a skillet or wok. Cook garlic and shallots until soft and brown. Add mushrooms and cook until beginning to brown. Add beans, salt and pepper. Cook on high heat for 3–4 minutes, turning constantly.

Tempeh with Balsamic Glaze
Serve with Pan-Roasted Potatoes and Autumn Spiced Red Cabbage

This delicious, simple dish is not only hearty and satisfying, but is low in fat, high in protein and totally gluten free. Tempeh is a soybean product that is formed into a firm, rectangular block. It is easy to work with and has a nutty flavor. It is available in health food stores and supermarkets and comes in a variety of flavors. It can be used in chili and soups, as the main ingredient in sandwiches and as an entrée. I have suggested two colorful side dishes. Use your imagination on this one. Try adding your favorite veggies and sauces. With the potatoes and cabbage, this serves 4–6.

2 packages tempeh (8 oz. each)

2 Tbl. olive oil

2 garlic cloves, minced

6 button mushrooms, thinly sliced

2 Tbl. balsamic vinegar

1/3 cup orange juice

1 Tbl. honey

Sea salt and ground black pepper

2 tsp. cornstarch

2/3 cup water

1 Tbl. chopped Italian parsley

Cut each tempeh block into 12 pieces. Heat oil in a skillet, add garlic and cook until soft and brown. Add tempeh and mushrooms and cook until mushrooms are soft. Turn tempeh and cook until browned on both sides.
Mix together vinegar, orange juice, honey and salt and pepper. Dissolve cornstarch in water and add to vinegar. Pour into skillet and cook until mixture begins to thicken. Sprinkle on the chopped parsley and continue to turn tempeh gently for another minute. Place on a platter and garnish with sprigs of fresh parsley.

Pan-Roasted Potatoes

12 small new potatoes, washed, trimmed
  and quartered
4 Tbl. butter
1½ Tbl. chopped fresh rosemary
Sea salt and black pepper to taste

Generously butter a roasting pan. Place potatoes
in pan, dot with 2 Tbl. butter and sprinkle with
rosemary, salt and pepper to coat thoroughly.
Pour in ¼ cup water. Cover pan and cook for
30 minutes. Uncover, stir and dot with another
2 Tbl. butter. Cook for 10 minutes more or until
potatoes are soft and browned. To crisp up, place
pan under the broiler for a few minutes.

Garnish with sprigs of fresh rosemary.

Autumn Spiced Red Cabbage

*This dressing is similar to the one in the recipe
for Pickled Beets, but with a few more spices.
The longer this sits, the better it tastes.*

6 cups chopped red cabbage
½ cup cider vinegar
2 cups water
¼ cup white sugar
Pinch of salt
1 tsp. ground cloves
½ tsp. grated nutmeg
1 cinnamon stick

In a heavy pot, combine all ingredients and boil
until cabbage is tender, about 45 minutes. Discard
cinnamon stick and serve hot.

Growing up, we always had homemade sweets in our lunchboxes, and dinner was not complete without a home-baked dessert. My mother loved to bake, and she would clip recipes from the Chat page of *The Boston Globe* that had been submitted by housewives from all over New England. I still have those recipes, many of which started with a personal greeting, like the banana bread recipe from Country Mom that began, "It's a great temptation for me to open my *Globe* and go right to the Chat section, so I have disciplined myself to wade through world problems first and then reap my reward." On a rare day home from school, I'd see my mother doing just that. She'd be settled at the big red kitchen table with the radio on, her coffee beside her, clipping recipes from the paper and gluing them into her recipe folder. It was a labor of love that came to fruition in luscious cakes and cookies.

After all these years, I still get a warm feeling when a particular scent brings back the memory of a special snow day. I had spent all day outside playing with my sisters Joanne and Kathleen and shoveling snow with my father. Exhausted and cold, we tumbled happily into the warm kitchen filled with mouth-watering aromas. My mother had baked a batch of apple muffins with a crunchy cinnamon topping that melted the chill away. So, go ahead and create an enduring memory for the people you love.

Breads & Pastries
Arann & Pastaetha

Irish Soda Bread

My mother's recipe card credits Sheila Burke with this version of Irish soda bread. Sheila was my father's first cousin and the sister of Sean O'Siochan, Director General of the GAA. In 1957, Sheila and her husband Michael came to America and stayed for 10 years. Michael worked at the Brockton Ice Company, and Sheila worked for my father at his store—James Patrick Sheehan's Religious Articles.

This recipe is what Irish Americans think of as "soda bread." However, this is not the soda bread of choice in Ireland, where the term refers to both white and brown bread, although the latter is most common. This bread is easy to make and ready in an hour. So here it is, the Sheehan family's Irish soda bread. Eat hot with lots of butter.

3 cups plain white flour

½ cup white sugar

1 cup raisins

1 Tbl. caraway seeds

½ tsp. salt

1 Tbl. baking powder

2 Tbl. butter

1 cup whole milk

Preheat oven to 350°. In a big bowl, mix all dry ingredients. Add the butter and, using your hands, crumble it in until thoroughly combined. Slowly add milk and mix together, adding more as needed until batter holds together well enough to be formed into a round loaf. Mark with a cross and bake on a greased baking sheet for 45 minutes or until a cake tester comes out clean. This will make a medium-sized loaf that can be cut into 8–12 pieces. Double the recipe to make a large loaf.

Irish Brown Bread

This simple brown bread is a staple of kitchens around Ireland. Imagine this baking in a round cast-iron pot over a turf fire.

1½ cups plain white flour

1½ cups stone-ground whole wheat flour

3 cups wheat bran

1 tsp. baking soda (bread soda)

1 tsp. baking powder

3 Tbl. dark brown sugar

1 egg

3 cups buttermilk

Preheat oven to 350°. In a big bowl, mix dry ingredients. Beat the egg with the buttermilk, add to dry ingredients and mix well. Pour into a large greased loaf pan or a 10" round cake pan. Bake for 40 minutes or until done.

Scones

Every morning at Mary's Café, we'd bake a batch of large scones filled with fresh or dried fruits, spices, nuts or—our most popular—chocolate chips! But, like the soda bread, scones are very different in Ireland. They are traditionally smaller, lighter in texture and filled with currants or raisins. The Whole Grain Brown Scones are a nice hearty variation, and the extra-coarse stone-ground flour gives them a nutty taste and texture.

Big Bold American Scones

> 5 cups plain white flour
> 1 cup white sugar
> 2 Tbl. baking powder
> 1 tsp. salt
> ½ cup cold butter
> 2 eggs
> 1 to 1½ cups whole milk

Preheat oven to 350°. Mix dry ingredients in a bowl. Cut butter into small pieces and add to dry ingredients, working in with your hands or pulsing in a food processor until crumbly. Beat eggs with milk and add to bowl. Add approximately 1 cup fresh or dried fruit. Drop dough onto a greased baking sheet and bake for 30 minutes or until done. This recipe makes 8 large or 12 small scones.

Other Suggestions:
Apple Spice Scones: Before baking, top scones with a swirl of thinly sliced peeled apples and sprinkle with a mixture of grated nutmeg, cinnamon and demerara sugar.

Fresh Cranberry Scones: Add whole cranberries to dough and top with grated orange peel and demerara sugar.

Traditional Irish Scones

How lovely to sit and relax in the garden with a proper cup of tea and a scone with homemade jam.
Thanks to Christina McGuane from the Perfumery shop for this lovely scone recipe.

    6 cups self-raising plain white flour
    1 tsp. baking powder
    1 cup white sugar
    6 Tbl. cold butter
    2 eggs
    1 to 1½ cups buttermilk
    1 cup currants

Preheat oven to 350°. Mix dry ingredients in a bowl. Cut butter into small pieces and add to dry ingredients. Work in with your hands or pulse in a food processor until crumbly. Beat eggs with milk and add to bowl. Add currants and combine well.

Flour a level surface such as a countertop or cutting board. On the floured surface, spread dough into a ½"-thick round. Use a rolling pin to even it out and make it smooth. With a 3" round mold, cut out 12 scones. Grease a baking sheet and bake for 30 minutes or until done.

Whole Grain Brown Scones

The nutty texture of a good stone-ground brown flour adds flavor and substance to this breakfast treat.

2 cups stone-ground brown flour
2 cups plain white flour
1 Tbl. dark brown sugar
1 tsp. salt
1 tsp. baking soda (bread soda)
4 Tbl. cold butter
¾ to 1 cup buttermilk

Preheat oven to 350°. Mix dry ingredients in a bowl. Cut butter into small pieces and add to dry ingredients. Work in with your hands or pulse in a food processor until crumbly. Beat eggs with milk and add to bowl.

Flour a surface such as a cutting board or countertop. Spread the dough into a ½"-thick round. Roll out to make dough smooth and even. With a 3" round mold, cut out approximately 8 scones. Grease a baking sheet and bake for 30 minutes or until done.

The Butter Road
A story of survival from the family history, as told by my grandfather

" My grandparents, Concubhar O'Siochain and Maire Ni Muineachain, lived in Kilgarvan, County Kerry. They had five sons and one daughter. My grandfather died when their youngest child, Connie, was only a year old.

My grandmother carried on the work of the farm with her young family. Her nearest butter market was in Cork city, 50 miles from Kilgarvan. Twice a month, she took her butter to the market, walking both ways. After milking her cows in the evening, she would start that long journey, arriving at the market in the morning and returning in time for the evening milking."

I traveled the Butter Road with my cousin Liam to check his turf on the Musheragh Mountains. It was a hot, sunny day, and as I looked out over the valley, I wondered how our great-great grandmother carried the wooden barrel of butter over this mountain. Did she have a donkey and cart? Did she walk alone? Did she rest on the Kerryman's Table, this ancient standing stone? As a young widow and mother, how did Maire and her children survive the famine that affected 3 million Irish lives through starvation and emigration and drove her two eldest sons to America?

This other Mary Sheehan, so strong and resilient, connects me to this land and the indomitable Irish spirit.

Soy Flax Bread

This is a gluten-free, non-dairy yeast bread that is highly nutritious. Xanthan gum is a necessary stabilizer in gluten-free yeast breads that is available in health food stores. Flax seeds are high in fiber and omega-3 fatty acids, which are good for the heart and possess anti-cancer properties. The combination of flours that I use here work nicely in other recipes that call for a gluten-free mix. This makes a big loaf with a nice brown crust. Make the full amount and refrigerate for future use.

2 cups white rice flour	½ cup warm water
1/3 cup potato flour	1½ Tbl. yeast
1/3 cup soy flour	2/3 cup plain soy milk
1/3 cup tapioca flour	¼ cup soy margarine
3½ tsp. xanthan gum	1¼ cups water
3 Tbl. ground flax seeds	1 tsp. white vinegar
	3 eggs

Preheat oven to 350°. Combine flours, xanthan gum and flax seeds in a mixer. In a small bowl, dissolve yeast in warm water. To help activate yeast, add a pinch of white sugar. Cover with plastic wrap and set aside until mixture gets bubbly, about 10 minutes.

Melt the margarine in 1¼ cups water. To dry ingredients add margarine, soy milk, water and vinegar. Slowly beat in eggs. Add the yeast mixture and beat on high speed for a few minutes. This dough will be loose, unlike bread dough made with wheat flour.

Put dough in a bowl, cover with a towel and set in a warm place for 1½ hours until doubled in size. Spoon batter into a large, greased loaf pan. Bake for 40–50 minutes.

Steamed Brown Fruit Bread

This recipe combines features of Irish tea brac, steamed Boston brown bread and date nut bread. It is delicious and good for you! You can make it gluten free by substituting a gluten-free flour mix for the flours. The bread is steamed in a can on the stovetop and is wonderful served in thick slices smothered with cream cheese. Refrigerated, it will keep for 2 weeks.

1½ cups whole wheat flour
1 cup white flour
1 cup cornmeal
1½ tsp. baking powder
½ tsp. baking soda (bread soda)
1 tsp. salt
½ cup raisins
1 cup chopped dates
½ cup sunflower seeds
¼ cup sesame seeds
½ cup chopped walnuts
½ cup molasses
¼ cup honey
2 cups whole milk

In a big bowl, mix ingredients in order using a wooden spoon. Fill 2 greased coffee cans with batter. Cover with aluminum foil. Place cans in a large pot with enough boiling water to come halfway up the sides of the cans. Cover pot with lid. Keep the water boiling, adding more as it evaporates. Steam for 2 hours. Remove from pot, take aluminum foil off and cool. The bread will slip out of the can when cooled.

Apricot and Almond Orange Bread

This is a sweet and tangy bread that can be served for breakfast, for tea, or even as a dessert. Make little loaves, tie colorful ribbons around them and give them as special homemade gifts for the holidays.

1½ cups chopped dried apricots

1 cup orange juice

½ cup water

2 Tbl. butter

1 egg

1 tsp. almond extract

1 cup white sugar

1 tsp. salt

1 tsp. baking soda (bread soda)

1½ cups plain white flour

1 cup whole wheat flour

½ cup chopped almonds

Preheat oven to 350°. Place apricots, orange juice, water and butter in a pot and bring to a boil. Remove from pot, put in a mixing bowl and let cool. Mix together all dry ingredients. When apricots have cooled, add egg and almond extract and beat well. Slowly add dry ingredients. The batter will be thick.

Grease and flour a large loaf pan. Pour batter into pans and top with chopped almonds. Bake for 45–50 minutes or until done.

Chocolate Oatmeal Nut Cookies

This recipe calls for lots of ingredients, but it makes a big, beautiful cookie that will totally satisfy that chocolate urge.

1 cup butter
1 cup white sugar
1 cup brown sugar
1½ tsp. vanilla extract
2 eggs
2 cups plain white flour
2½ cups oats (not instant)
½ tsp. salt
1 tsp. baking soda (bread soda)
1 Tbl. baking powder
2 tsp. instant coffee granules
4 oz. semi-sweet chocolate broken into
   small pieces
12 oz. semi-sweet chocolate chips
1½ cups chopped walnuts, pecans, or
   macadamia nuts

Preheat oven to 350°. Cream butter and sugars until fluffy. Mix in vanilla and eggs. In another bowl, mix together flour, oats, salt, soda, baking powder and coffee granules. Add the chocolate pieces, chips and nuts. Add flour mixture to wet ingredients and mix thoroughly. Drop round spoonfuls onto a greased cookie sheet and bake for 12–15 minutes or until cookies begin to brown. Cookies harden as they cool, so don't overcook.

Eat as many as you want with a big glass of milk.

Carrot Cake

Cream cheese icing makes this carrot cake irresistible.

1 cup vegetable oil
1 cup white sugar
3 eggs
1 tsp. vanilla extract
3 cups peeled, shredded carrots
1 cup sifted plain white flour
1 cup whole wheat flour
1 tsp. salt
2 tsp. baking soda (bread soda)
1½ tsp. cinnamon
Optional: ½ cup raisins

Cream Cheese Icing:
8 oz. soft cream cheese
¼ cup soft butter
½ tsp. vanilla extract
1 lb. powdered sugar (icing sugar,
    confectioners' sugar)

Blend cream cheese and butter until smooth. Add vanilla and slowly mix in powdered sugar.

Preheat oven to 350°. Cream oil and sugar. Beat in eggs and vanilla. Add carrots. To wet ingredients add flours, salt, baking soda and cinnamon. Fold in walnuts and raisins (if used). Grease and flour a 10" cake pan and pour batter into pan. Bake for 35–40 minutes or until done. Cool and remove from pan. Ice and decorate with whole walnuts.

Chocolate Cake

This moist, light cake is dairy free and uses no eggs, so it is great for our vegan friends. I have given a dairy-free icing option as well.

1 cup white sugar
1½ cups self-raising white flour
½ tsp. salt
¼ cup dark cocoa
1 Tbl. white vinegar
½ cup vegetable oil
1 tsp. vanilla extract
1 cup cold water

Chocolate Icing:
2 oz. butter
4 Tbl. semi-sweet dark chocolate
3 Tbl. milk
5 oz. powdered sugar

Non-dairy Chocolate Icing:
2 oz. margarine
4 Tbl. semi-sweet non-dairy dark chocolate
3 Tbl. plain soy milk
5 oz. powdered sugar

Preheat oven to 350°. Mix together dry ingredients. Slowly add vinegar, oil, vanilla and water until well combined. Grease and flour an 8" cake pan. Bake for 25–30 minutes. Cool, remove from pan and ice.

For either icing:
Chop chocolate into small pieces. In a heavy pot, melt butter and add chocolate. Cook on low heat, stirring constantly, until chocolate melts. Remove pan from stove and cool. Put milk and sugar in a mixer, blend and add cooled chocolate to mixture. Beat until fluffy.

Cinnamon Swirl Coffee Cake

This is an old recipe that my mother used to make for special occasions. It is delightful with afternoon tea.

½ cup butter
1 cup white sugar
2 eggs
1 tsp. vanilla extract
2 cups sifted plain white flour
½ tsp. salt
1 tsp. baking soda (bread soda)
1 tsp. baking powder
1 cup sour cream

Cinnamon-Walnut Filling and Topping:
Mix together:
¼ cup light brown sugar
1 tsp. cinnamon
½ cup crushed walnuts

Preheat oven to 350°. Cream butter and sugar until light and fluffy. Add eggs and vanilla and mix well. Slowly add flour, then salt, soda and baking powder. Fold in sour cream and mix well.

Grease and flour a 10" cake pan or tube pan. Spread half the batter in the pan. Sprinkle with half the filling. Top with the rest of the batter and sprinkle on the rest of the filling. Bake for 50–60 minutes or until done.

Tarts

Ireland has not only wonderful organic vegetables, but also delicious organic fruits. In June, gardens are red with plump, juicy strawberries. Rhubarb grows from May to August, and apple orchards are in bloom summer and fall. This Pastry Dough recipe is an all-purpose one that I use for quiche and double pie crusts.

Pastry Dough

> 5 cups plain white flour
> Pinch of salt
> 1½ cups cold butter or 1 cup butter and ½ cup shortening
> 12–14 Tbl. cold water

Sift flour with salt. Cut cold butter into small pieces. Measure 5 cups flour and, in a bowl or food processor, mix in butter until the dough becomes crumbly. Slowly add cold water until dough can be formed into a smooth ball. Wrap in wax paper and refrigerate for at least 1 hour. Cut dough in half. (Roll out other half for a top crust or refrigerate for up to 1 week.) Flour a flat surface and spread out dough. With a rolling pin, roll dough into a 10" round and place in a tart or pie dish. Crimp edges. Makes two 10" pies or a single pie with a top crust.

Strawberry Rhubarb Tart

Perfect together—the tartness of rhubarb paired with the sweetness of strawberries.

Combine, in the following order:
　　3 cups rhubarb, cut into 1" pieces
　　2 cups sliced strawberries
　　¼ cup plain white flour
　　1¼ cup white sugar
　　1 Tbl. freshly squeezed lemon juice
　　½ tsp. grated nutmeg

Crumb Topping:
1 cup chopped walnuts
1 cup light brown sugar
2/3 cup plain white flour
1 tsp. cinnamon
½ cup oats (not instant)
8 Tbl. cold butter, cut into small pieces

Preheat oven to 350°.

Prepare crumb topping by mixing dry ingredients and adding butter pieces until mixture is crumbly.

Line a 10" tart pan with Pastry Dough. Pour the fruit mixture into pan. Top with crumb topping or a lattice crust made from the Pastry Dough. Bake for 40 minutes. Serve with a dollop of fresh cream.

Apple Cranberry Tart

Impress guests with this colorful autumn dessert that is a perfect ending to a holiday dinner.

5 cups sweet apples, peeled, cored and sliced
1 cup whole fresh cranberries
1 Tbl. freshly squeezed lemon juice
1 cup white sugar
1½ Tbl. plain white flour
½ tsp. grated nutmeg
1 tsp. cinnamon
1 Tbl. minced fresh ginger root
2 Tbl. cold butter

Preheat oven to 350°. Toss apples and cranberries with lemon juice and sugar. Mix thoroughly. Add flour and spices and place in a 10" tart pan. Dot small pieces of cold butter evenly over filling. Top with a crust or crumb topping. Bake for 45–50 minutes. Serve hot with vanilla ice cream.

Vegan Pumpkin Pie

I've been blessed to make wonderful friends through my cooking, among them Martha and Walter Gamble. You'd never guess they were octogenarians—due to many years of a macrobiotic diet, daily yoga practice, good humor and peace-making, they are the picture of good health. Many thanks to them for this delicious dairy-free pie recipe.

Arrowroot powder comes from the root of a West Indian plant. It is gluten free and is used as a thickening agent in baked goods, sauces and soups.

3½ cups mashed pumpkin

2 cups plain soy milk

¼ cup arrowroot powder

½ to ¾ cup maple syrup

1 Tbl. vanilla extract

½ tsp. cinnamon

½ tsp. grated nutmeg

½ tsp. salt

Preheat oven to 350°. Mix all ingredients until thoroughly combined. Pour into a 9" pie shell. Bake for 50–60 minutes.

Mary's Dog Biscuits

I created these healthy snacks for Annie, Raven, and The Dude. Now they are the favorite treats of all my furry friends on both sides of the Pond. Wheat berries are whole, unprocessed wheat kernels. They are high in protein and fiber. Because these biscuits contain cooked fresh veggies and grains, they will need to be refrigerated for a longer shelf-life.

2 cups whole wheat flour

1½ cups plain white flour

1 Tbl. sunflower seeds

1 Tbl. flax seeds

¼ cup wheat bran or wheat germ

¼ cup cooked wheat berries or spelt

1 cup chopped celery and carrots, cooked

1 egg

1 cup veggie stock

Preheat oven to 350 . In a mixer, combine all dry ingredients. Add wheat berries, veggies and eggs. Slowly pour in the stock and mix until dough is firm. Flour a level surface and roll the batter out to a ½" thickness. Using dog bone molds (2" for small bones or 3½" for large bones), cut into shapes, place on a greased cookie sheet and bake for 35 minutes.

This recipe makes 50 small or 12 large biscuits.

Conversion Charts

Volume Conversions: Liquids

Customary quantity	Metric equivalent
1 teaspoon	5 mL
1 tablespoon or 1/2 fluid ounce	15 mL
1 fluid ounce or 1/8 cup	30 mL
1/4 cup or 2 fluid ounces	60 mL
1/3 cup	80 mL
1/2 cup or 4 fluid ounces	120 mL
2/3 cup	160 mL
3/4 cup or 6 fluid ounces	180 mL
1 cup or 8 fluid ounces or half a pint	240 mL
1 1/2 cups or 12 fluid ounces	350 mL
2 cups or 1 pint or 16 fluid ounces	475 mL
3 cups or 1 1/2 pints	700 mL
4 cups or 2 pints or 1 quart	950 mL
4 quarts or 1 gallon	3.8 L

Note: In cases where higher precision is not justified, it may be convenient to round these conversions off as follows:

1 cup = 250 mL
1 pint = 500 mL
1 quart = 1 L
1 gallon = 4 L

Weight Conversions

Customary quantity	Metric equivalent
1 ounce	28 g
4 ounces or 1/4 pound	113 g
1/3 pound	150 g
8 ounces or 1/2 pound	230 g
2/3 pound	300 g
12 ounces or 3/4 pound	340 g
1 pound or 16 ounces	450 g
2 pounds	900 g

Length Conversions

Customary quantity	Metric equivalent
1/8 inch	3 mm
1/4 inch	6 mm
1/2 inch	13 mm
3/4 inch	19 mm
1 inch	2.5 cm
2 inches	5 cm
3 inches	7.6 cm

Oven Temperatures

Farenheit	Centigrade
350° F	175° C
375° F	190° C
400° F	205° C

Photographs

Index

DF = dairy-free; GF = gluten-free

Index *(continued)*

A Love Story
From my grandfather's family history

" When I was appointed Gaelic Teacher and Organizer for the town of Dingle I had occasion to visit the Curran family often, as Annie's brother John was secretary. On my first visit I was impressed with the beautiful dark haired girl who was the first to greet me. Her charming personality and stately bearing made a lasting impression on me. Afterwards, when I met her at the Gaelic classes my admiration increased. In selecting a cast for the play "An Doctuir", which we had in connection to the Feis, I gave Annie the leading part. My part in the play was her husband. That was the beginning of a beautiful romance.

"Knowing that she had many admirers and would receive a good dowry from her parents I realized that she was making too much of a sacrifice in being interested in one who had only a small salary as a traveling teacher, shifting from one place to another.

"In 1906, I had a letter from my brother, John, urging me to come to America, that I would do well here. I was surprised as I had never expressed any desire to leave Ireland. However, I gave this offer serious thought and made an appointment to see Annie.

"During that meeting she said she believed it was the answer to our prayers, and she would go to any part of the world with me. I felt flattered that a girl so good and beautiful as she was, with all the advantages of a happy home and excellent prospects of a good marriage near her own people should want to give them up for the hardships of life with a poor boy in a foreign country. We decided to go to America—the great land of opportunities."

Where to Buy This Book

Coming Home to Cook is available at www.marysheehan.com

To contact the author, please email Mary Sheehan at mary_sheehan@comcast.net.